To Ann with best wishes
John Fiske

Yours Sincerely

Also by John Fiske (with Lisa Freeman)

Living with Early Oak: Seventeenth-Century English Furniture Then and Now (Belmont Press)

Yours Sincerely

Essays on Antiques and Country Life

John Fiske

Illustrations by Robert Sydorowich

The Belmont Press
Belmont, Vermont

© 2006 John Fiske and Lisa Freeman. All rights reserved.

ISBN: 0-9754569-1-1

The Belmont Press
PO Box 270
Belmont, Vermont 05730
802.259.2579
802.259.3065 fax
info@fiskeandfreeman.com
www.fiskeandfreeman.com

Designed and produced by Lisa Freeman (www.lfreemanmarketing.com).

CONTENTS

List of Illustrations	vii
Preface	ix
January	
Mick	3
Humble History	7
February	
Homeland Security	13
Hip	16
March	
Trees	23
Transitions	27
April	
Mending Wall	33
Immigrants	37
May	
Weather	43
Angel	46
June	
Square Dance	53
Dinner	56

July
- Parade ... 63
- Independence ... 67

August
- Just Us ... 73
- Small Adults ... 77

September
- The Real US ... 83
- Cider Days ... 86

October
- Darkness ... 93
- Kitchen ... 96

November
- Sayings ... 103
- Clearing ... 107

December
- Ping Pong ... 113
- Feasting ... 116

LIST OF ILLUSTRATIONS

Ascutney	1
Gristmill	11
Sap Buckets	21
East Corinth	31
Spring Flowers	41
Bethel	51
Patriot	61
Concert	71
Hay Bales	81
Long Trail	91
Suzy	101
Christmas Card	111

To Lucy, and her new life
To Matthew, who should have lived longer
To Lisa, who is my life

PREFACE

Dear Reader,

Tucked away in the Green Mountains of Vermont lies Belmont, a small village in the town of Mount Holly. It's where I live with Lisa, my wife, and with our wonderful golden retriever and two Maine coon cats. I was born in England, but now I'm American. I used to be a university professor, but now I'm the editor of the *New England Antiques Journal*, an antiques dealer, and a bit of a curmudgeon with a very soft heart.

    These essays were first published in the *New England Antiques Journal*, though I've edited them a little to make them suitable for a book. If you enjoy them, as I sincerely hope you will, you can read a new one every month on the back page of the *Journal*.

All of my colleagues at the *New England Antiques Journal* deserve my gratitude, but I'd like to thank in particular Pat Turley for giving me scope, John Grogan for making sure it all works, Mary Hahn without whom it couldn't possibly work, Noah Fleisher who works alongside me every step of the way, and Mark Ehrlich for such long support and friendship that it doesn't seem like work.

And then there's Lisa: she's at the center of everything I write, think, and do, even if I'm the only one who can see her there.

And of course, there's you, my readers. Thank you for welcoming me into your homes.

Yours sincerely,

John Fiske

MICK

Mick Seward died last week. He was the third generation of Sewards to farm the lands around our house, and luckily, his son Art, his nephew Dave, and Art's son Andrew are all determined that the farm will survive to the fourth generation. That's as rare as hens' teeth in Vermont these days. In 1980, our town alone had 35 farms, now we have one. Things change. Sometimes too quickly.

Mick died too quickly, too. He was seventy, still young for an old-timer. He was standing on a stone wall, lopping off a branch with a chain saw, and lost his balance. As he fell, he threw the saw away from him, but it kicked back and took a chunk out of his leg. He walked back to the farm and had his wife Louise dress the wound, but he wouldn't let her take him to the E.R. Oh dear. After a bone infection, skin grafts, and ten days with his leg in a hoist, he had the heart attack that finally killed him. There was no funeral, Mick didn't hold with them. They buried his ashes under the tree he'd chosen, in the meadow they call "top o' the farm."

He'll be there for ever, in the land that he loved and cursed with equal intensity. Every spring, after plowing, Mick would drive the tractor with the front-end loader, and Art and Dave would walk ahead with pry-bars loosening the rocks that the plow had brought to the surface so that Mick could scoop them up. Cursing and loving. As Mick used to say, "In six days God made the world, and on the seventh he rested – and threw rocks at Vermont."

Those cursed rocks make our beloved stone walls. The walls creep up and across our hillsides, dividing our meadows and cutting pointlessly through the woodlands that were good grazing only a generation or two ago. They carry the calloused history of the men like Mick who cleared the land and made it productive. These men also made Vermont beautiful, they created our landscape of meadows and plowlands and forests, and, of course, stone walls.

Our town's historical society has started photographing and inventorying our stone walls, and our conservation group is trying to preserve some of the lands on which they lie. I'm active in both. Working with them complements nicely my work with antiques. Working with stone walls and landscapes and antiques is working with the sort of history I love. It's what I call "humble history." It's not written in books, it's not stored in huge archives in the Library of Congress. It's the history of ordinary folk, and it's written in the things they used and the things they did.

It's wrong for us to look down on the humble history of men like Mick. Mick grew up in a Vermont that was different. He changed as much as he had to, but he didn't like change, and he kept the old ways as long as he could make them work, sometimes longer than he should. He was stubborn, and he never allowed anyone else to think for him, even when he was wrong – no, especially when he was wrong. His farmyard was full of modern machinery – the farm wouldn't have survived without it – but Mick never let modern machines change the man he was and the way he lived. Ironically, it was a chain saw that killed him, a chain saw and a stone wall.

Now, we're all high-tech, high-consumerist, high-speed: if we don't change everything twice a year, we're out of date. It's the way we have to be to live in today's world. But our forebears had to be what they had to be to live in theirs. Humble history does not – it emphatically does not – show us how far we have "advanced" from such "primitive" beginnings. Humble history tells us that people who were fundamentally like us lived productive, satisfying lives in ways that were very different from ours. Humble history reminds us that the way we live now is not the only way, and not necessarily the best way, for human beings to live. It stops us from being arrogant, it prevents us from being complacent. Humble history is the memory of living differently, but well. That's why so many of us want to keep antiques, and stone walls, and the memory of old-timers as important parts of our lives today. For us, Mick Seward isn't dead.

HUMBLE HISTORY

Over lunch, I'll read the Rutland Herald, and in the evenings, I'll often watch a bit of CNN. I live in a 150-year old farmhouse filled with antiques, dogs, a Maine Coon cat, and a beautiful wife. And it all reminds me of the two quite different sorts of history that infuse our lives.

I watch history-making on the TV – generals and admirals, presidents of this and that, secretary-generals of something else, ministers of finance, foreign affairs, fisheries, and food. Then I look at my grandmother's copper beer jug, and I'm reminded that ordinary folk make history, too. But theirs is a history that's not covered by the media, not recorded in millions of official documents in millions of filing cabinets. It's recorded in memories, and it's recorded in antiques.

As a young man, my grandfather planted thirty acres of apple trees. Those trees became his life and his livelihood. Every July, a gang of mowers would come with their scythes to cut the hay around the trees. They'd work their way northward, following the ripening hay up the east coast of England – imagine scything your way for two hundred miles, six inches at a stoke, bent double. Then, in the fall, they'd shoulder their scythes and walk back south to their homes. At lunchtime my grandmother would take them beer in her big copper jug, and they'd sit under the trees to drink it. That jug is no longer full of beer, but of memories. It's a little piece of ordinary, humble history. Humble history can be frustrating because memories don't last in the way that documents do.

We've just bought a wonderful farmhouse chair, made about 300 years ago. Small frames protrude from each side of the back to form wings. The farmer would have draped a cloth around them and drawn the chair up to a blazing fire. The fire would have toasted his front, and the cloth would have kept the drafts from his back and his stockinged feet.

The winters in the north of Old England were cold, not New England cold, but cold enough. In both countries, a huge log fire was the only source of heat. The more brightly it roared, the more heat it gave, and the colder the drafts it sucked in through every gap in the door frame, through every crack in the clapboards. The farmer needed that cloth around the back of his chair.

But nobody has recorded what sort of cloth it was. Was it his heavy, farm-dirty cloak? Or had his wife simply stitched some empty flour sacks together? Had she treated her husband to a length of homespun or even real woven material bought on one of their rare trips to Halifax or York? Had she sewn loops to fit over the finials? We just don't know.

We know too much of the big, official history that CNN and Fox News broadcast 24/7, and too little of the humble history of folks like us, but without this humble history, the big history has no flesh and blood. Antiques are the documents of humble history. I offer no prizes for guessing which sort of history means the most to me.

FEBRUARY

HOMELAND SECURITY

I've just been photographed and entered into the Homeland Security Digital Database. Now, the database may well be a good thing, and may well be central in the war against terror, but it sure feels eerie knowing that I'm in it.

We were doing a show in Washington D.C., and to cut down on expenses, we were staying south of the Potomac in Virginia, close to the Iwo Jima monument. We were also, unbeknownst to me, close to the Pentagon. In the wake of 9/11, the local traffic patterns around the Pentagon had all been redrawn by security planners. Some streets were one-way, many banned trucks, but our map gave no indication of these restrictions. Consequently, we found ourselves driving our truck on a "no-trucks" highway just in front of the Pentagon. The police found us, too. We were stopped within moments of getting onto the highway, our IDs checked by computer, the truck searched (luckily, we'd unloaded and had only a back-up piece in there), and we were then directed to another unmarked car lurking in the bushes, where I was photographed.

At least I brought some variety to their database. I doubt if it contains many bald-headed Englishmen wearing natty bow ties and dressed up to the nines, even if I was driving a diesel truck just across the street from the Pentagon.

Once they had determined that Lisa and I were unlikely to destroy the U.S. Armed Forces, the police gave us (very complicated) directions for driving north through downtown Washington to the show. We followed them as best we could and turned onto Constitution Avenue, only to be confronted once again with one of those dreaded "no trucks" signs. And, simultaneously, by a cop. One more ID check, one more truck search – but no photo this time. This cop even looked in the drawers of the secretary in the back. Now that's an idea – a drawer-bomb! Those people who wander aimlessly through the booth, idly pulling out every drawer that they pass without interrupting their intense gossiping – they'd reach Drawer Code Zero, and KABOOM – vaporized!!

But, back to reality. We had our own homeland security crisis to take care of. Someone in the village noticed gigantic icicles on our house where icicles had never been seen before and where they surely didn't oughta be now. An ice dam on the eaves had forced melting snow into the soffit. These people didn't know us well, so they contacted our close friends, John and Gail, who climbed up into our attic to see if the water was getting inside. Luckily it wasn't. They called us to explain the problem, and we called Chad, whose father Doug plows our driveway. Within an hour, Chad was up on our roof attacking the ice dam and saving us from the invasion of snow melt.

I'm glad that we're organizing our national Homeland Security, complete with undriveable traffic patterns, digital cameras, and a huge electronic database. But I'm so much more comfortable with the homeland security that comes from neighbors looking out for neighbors. I feel at home in Vermont, but an alien in Washington. And I'd never stuff an antique with gunpowder!

HIP

I'm writing this lying flat on my back with my ankles eighteen inches apart and my toes pointing straight at the ceiling. Those of you who have been in the same boat will recognize that I have just had a hip replaced. My room is comfortable, clean, and equipped with everything I need, but it is visually the most boring room I've ever been in.

Like all antique collectors, I'm not used to visual boredom – the rooms in which I live and feel at home are full of visual stimulation, beautiful and interesting objects everywhere, a clutter of things to look at.

The blandness of my hospital room led to a request that even Lisa found bizarre, and she's been married to my oddities long enough to be pretty unfazed by any of them. I didn't want flowers to brighten up the room, I wanted an old wine bottle. It is now standing confidently on a little corner shelf opposite the foot of my bed. I love watching it fight against the neutral, boring colors on the walls and ceiling. It's winning!

Of course, it's not your grocery store wine bottle, and it doesn't even look like one. For a start, it's made of leather, which has stiffened, dried, crackled, and blackened over its four-hundred-year life span. And it's not bottle-shaped: it's like a big balled-up fist with three fingers rising vertically from it. One finger is about an inch in diameter and was used for filling the bottle from the cask. The middle is the smallest of the three, and the only one that is flat: at its top is a small hole from which to hang the bottle from a belt or a saddle-bag. The third is as long as the first, but narrower and pointed: at its end is a small hole from which a thin stream of wine squirted directly into the drinker's mouth – no need for an expensive and breakable wine glass.

It catches the eye of everyone who walks into the room. It is visually, historically, and imaginatively vibrant. They have to ask me about it; they have to touch it. It's currently my favorite item in our collection.

The other reason it works so well for me in this room is that it's real. It's a piece of reality as we used to understand it. So much of the equipment in the room is not real, but virtual. When the intern comes to see how I'm doing, he doesn't look at my real body, he looks at its virtual representation on a monitor. The jagged lines and bar charts and figures are what I really am to him. When the nurse comes to check my "vital signs," as she calls them, she sticks things on various bits of me and looks at the read-out on a screen. That's how she knows I'm alive.

I know that an electronic probe in my ear gives a far more accurate reading of my temperature than a soft hand on my brow; I know that a sensor on my finger records my pulse better than cold fingers on my wrist. But I regret the passing of the world of soft hands and cold fingers, a world in which people really touched each other to know each other. Our world is now one in which an electronic image has become more real than the real object it represents. It's crazy, but virtual reality has replaced old-fashioned "real" reality.

The leather wine bottle is intransigently real. It cannot be reduced to an electronic image. It absolutely, resolutely, refuses to be virtual. It comes from a time when real people drank real wine and never felt that their reality was inadequate, that it needed to be enhanced electronically so that they could understand it better. The wine bottle is what it is what it is, and that's all there is to it.

This blackened leather bottle challenges the monitor screen just as effectively as it challenges the visual blandness. That's why I wanted it. On reflection, I've come to realize that in its own way, our old wine bottle in this high-tech room is the equivalent of the titanium-and-ceramic hip in my old body. It takes an effort to bring the two worlds together and make them work as one, but it can be done. And that's the main job of an antique today.

TREES

Jeff and Pat Teter are tapping our maples. I didn't think they'd be able to this year. The last time I saw them was on TV: they were in Torino, at the Winter Olympics, watching their daughter Hannah win the gold medal in the women's half pipe. But here they are, just days after a once-in-lifetime event, engaging in a process that's as old as the hills in the background. Well, not quite – allow me a bit of poetic license. Native Americans taught the newly arrived English settlers how to tap maples for syrup: we have no idea how old the process actually is.

Sometimes I think sap runs through the veins of Vermonters – so close is the relationship between them and trees. Some years ago, we decided to move some young trees from our woods to the edge of the meadow on the side of the house to screen an ugly new house that that had just been plonked down in our view. I read all the right books, I followed their advice to the letter, and three out of four of my attempted transplants died. (I'm a transplant myself, I came from somewhere else, but I've put down roots, and I'm more than surviving, I'm thriving. Transplants, the human sort, will never be Vermonters, but we're a tad closer than the summer folk or the skiers.)

A transplant simply does not relate to trees in the way that a Vermonter does. The following year, we brought in a forester to do the transplanting for us. He was a young man, not long out of forestry school, tall, already a bit gnarly, and reticent. Thad walked up to the woods with Lisa and me. As we left the bright sun of the March meadow and entered the shade of the woodland, he suddenly came alive. He fondled each young tree, he talked animatedly about it. He told us how his professor would take the class into the school's woodlands and ask them to identify different species of trees and their variants. Thad was 100% correct, 100% of the time. But when the professor asked him to tell the rest of the class how he knew, Thad could only answer, "I just know." Thad and trees had grown up together, Vermonters both, and every one of the trees he transplanted is thriving well: they've almost hidden that house.

Wood is the basis of human society. It cooked our meals, warmed our bodies, provided our houses, tools, ships, and weapons. Sure, newer materials have taken over many of its functions, but they're never as fundamental as wood. Forced hot air is not a wood stove. Nobody runs their finger along a formica table top, but they can't help stroking the surface of an antique table. Touching well-worn wood is a way of reconnecting ourselves with something very basic. A wiser man than I has made the point that the age of wood has lasted for 10,000 years, whereas the age of coal and oil is a mere 250 years old, and its end is already in sight.

Jeff and Pat will boil the sap down to make their grade A syrup. That's all they have to do, boil 40 or 50 gallons of sap to make one gallon of syrup. A human process brings out the hidden essence of maple sap. Just as the craftsman 200 years ago planed and sanded maple boards so that he could bring out the hidden beauty of their grain and give it to the rest of us to enjoy. Human beings working with nature, whereas today, all too often, we work against her. That's why old-time craftsmanship matters so much: craftsmen work with nature, manufacturers impose upon her. And if we work against nature, we work against ourselves. No wonder there's so much disquiet among us.

So we humans are quietly driven to dip our fingers into new maple syrup and to run them along the top of the old maple farmhouse table. The same need drives us in each case, and it's the same thing that brought Jeff and Pat straight back to our maples from the dizzying heights of Torino. It's something to do with reconnecting. We recognize that wood and trees can put us back in touch, literally, with a reality we're frightened we've lost.

TRANSITIONS

On my way to Chicago, I nearly hit a girl moose. I assume she was the one who, a few days earlier, had ambled nonchalantly across our lawn blocking the light from the kitchen windows. She was young, a year or 18 months old perhaps, and looked as though she'd just been sent packing by her Mom, who now found the bull more interesting than her adolescent daughter. Or maybe not. What I know about the family life of moose could be written on the back of a postage stamp, as my grandmother used to say. But she did look kinda lonely.

With her head hanging low, she picked her way over the stone wall and out into the meadow where she stopped to browse just where the meadow ended and the woods began. She raised her ugly head and looked at me, as if to say, "OK, go on, take your durned photo, and leave me in peace." So I did, and I left her.

Nobody in their right mind can love a moose. They're over-sized, ill-proportioned, Stone Age creatures with not a single endearing habit as far as I can tell. Driving into one can be fatal, for their legs raise their 700-pound bodies to exactly the right height to come crashing through the windshield and into the front seat. My truck's a bit higher than that, but I still hit the brakes hard as I rounded a corner and found her hindquarters mooning at me just where the yellow line would have been if our little road had merited one.

I sat in the grey light of dawn and stared at her buttocks. She didn't care. Moose don't care, that's just the way they are. She kept me waiting until she decided that the woods suited her better than the middle of the road.

Now, I can't see much more to love about a city than a moose. But even I have to admit that the art nouveau skyscrapers on Chicago's Michigan Avenue are not exactly ugly. Neither was my destination. The building's Art Deco lobby was full of cool plasterwork, with niches holding white marble statues of those ultra-feminine, liquid-looking ladies that the period loved so much.

I was there to pick up a small collection of oak furniture that my client and his first wife had put together over 20 or 25 years of collecting. The second wife wanted it gone. Among the pieces was a two-seater settle, made of elm and walnut. It was too early to be called a love seat, but maybe they'd bought it to serve as one when their marriage was still strong: they were to be the latest in a long line of couples who had sat together on it. Divorce is good for antique dealers.

The first wife had gone who knows where; the antiques were coming to us; and the girl moose had wandered across our lawn. I hope the ex-wife finds someone to love her; I know we'll find customers to love the antiques; and I assume that my lugubrious moose will also find someone to fill her life with joy and laughter.

Moments of transition, when all our paths serendipitously met, crossed, and parted.

APRIL

MENDING WALL

> Something there is that doesn't love a wall,
> That sends the frozen-ground-swell under it,
> And spills the upper boulders in the sun.

I'm just a tad out of step with these lines by Robert Frost, Vermont's aptly named poet laureate (OK, I know New Hampshire claims him, too, but that's just wishful thinking!). I thank the frost that spills the upper boulders in the sun.

Vermont's stone walls touch me deeply, and I'm pleased that our second-home owners are rebuilding them around their remodeled and refurbished farm houses. But a rebuilt wall is a little like a stripped and refinished piece of furniture, it's too clean and neat. We have two or three expert stone masons in the village who build wonderful walls and patios for flatlanders. On many a Vermont road, there's a Vermont wall on one side and a flatlander wall on the other. In a flatlander wall, every stone is in its place, and the wall controls its surroundings, firmly dividing here from there. Vermont walls are part of their surroundings, and many a stone is out of its place. They're not in full control; here leaks into there.

Vermont walls were doubly functional. First, they were a place to stack the stones that had to be cleared every year from the meadows and fields. The same frost that brought the stones down from the wall brought new stones up in the fields. Then the walls of stacked stones worked to keep the cattle and the sheep from straying, and some of them marked the boundaries between one farm and the next. Frost doesn't understand this function too well, either,

> He is all pine and I am apple orchard.
> My apple trees will never get across
> And eat the cones under his pines, I tell him.
> He only says, "Good fences make good
> neighbors."

In England, up in the Peak District, I had a small mountain farm in limestone country. Every spring, I, too, would go "mending wall," and Frost's lines would run through my head as I went. There weren't specialist stone workers then, as there weren't in Vermont: farmers built and mended their own walls.

I remember one telling me, "A good waller never lifts a stone twice." A good waller eyed the gap in the wall, eyed the stones on the ground, and matched the two perfectly first time every time. I was not a good waller. I'd eye the gap, spot a stone to fit it, and then the durned thing would change shape in my hand, and I'd have to throw it down and try another.

But still I loved mending wall. It helped me fit myself into the cycle of the year, it made me part of nature's insistent reminder that we humans are never in full control of what we do and what we make. She always undoes something to make us do it again. For that's what she does, she grows, ripens, dies and sleeps, again and again and again. We think differently from nature: we like to believe that we move in a straight line going forward for ever. But nature moves in a cycle. Moving differently to her is not always to our advantage.

Our science and technology try to control nature as completely as possible. But the wise old bird has been around for too long to let us. Antique furniture's like stone walls. The joiner builds the sturdiest structure he can, and then in comes nature. She dries the wood and shrinks it, she twists the grain and warps it; she slides under the veneer and lifts it. She'll always remind us that we're not as smart as we think we are. Sometimes her reminders will be big, like a sea sweeping away a city: sometimes they'll be small, like a piece of veneer falling to the floor overnight. But always, eventually, she'll spill the upper boulders in the sun.

I suppose I'll like the flatlander walls better when they are less, dare I say it, flat. When nature has pushed a rock or two out of place, or heaved one section higher than another. That's why I prefer antique furniture to new: nature and humans have worked on it together. I'm sorry Robert, great poet that you are, nature does not dislike walls: she topples their upper boulders now and again just to remind us of who we are, and to put us back where we belong.

IMMIGRANTS

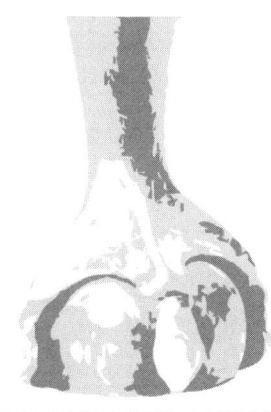

Our tiny town has the highest lake in Vermont. It's not very big, and it's no more beautiful than most lakes that are surrounded by hills. But we love it. It has a little swimming beach, and in the summer, we anchor a raft off it for the kids to dive from and push each other off. We have a summer festival with a barbecue, a band and silly canoe races, and we welcome the New Year with a bonfire on the beach. We love our lake.

Our lake is being choked by Eurasian Milfoil. This dreaded invader from Asia has no natural enemies, so it spreads like wildfire. We've had teams of volunteers pulling it by hand, we've bred special weevils who we're told like to eat it. But it outruns all our efforts. And the town can't afford chemical treatment. Milfoil came from Asia, and it's spoiling our corner of

Vermont. In a globalized world, natural ecosystems are endangered by alien intruders.

But culture is not like nature. Culture benefits from the alien. Like milfoil, the ball-and-claw foot came from Asia. It originated in China, as a dragon's claw holding a pearl, where it symbolized, I believe, wisdom and peace. From there it traveled to England, and from England to here. By now, it has lost almost all traces of its Chinese meanings and origin and has become an integral part of American culture.

Similarly, the hairy paw foot, which supports so many classical and Empire pieces made here in the early nineteenth century, came to us from Egypt via France. Napoleon's campaigns in North Africa introduced Sphinx-like motifs to France. The French Revolution and the American Revolution were seen as sisters in democracy, so in the Federal period, it was more patriotic to be influenced by France than by England. As a result, the hairy paw foot is also part of American heritage.

Even the eagle, that most American of American symbols, is in fact an immigrant. In the Federal period, not surprisingly, it was everywhere – proudly carved and gilded atop girandole mirrors, and intricately inlaid into mahogany furniture. But the eagle of American independence was once the eagle of the Roman Empire, which was then transposed into English and French style, where it symbolized the imperial power from which America had freed itself. Only then, did it become American.

I could go on. The Imari pattern on Ironstone and the blue willow on Staffordshire are blends of East and West. An American card table may well be made of mahogany from the Caribbean, satinwood from India, rosewood from Brazil, ebony from Africa, and hinges from England.

A healthy, vigorous culture absorbs influences from other cultures and uses them to grow and develop. Antiques are good examples of this. They remind us not only of our past, but also of our adaptability, of our capacity for growth and change. They are evidence of our ability to take something beautiful, regardless of where it came from, and use it to enrich our own culture. A reassuring lesson in a globalized world, where too many people see other cultures as threatening. Yet another reason why we love living with antiques.

MAY

WEATHER

May Day has just dawned, and the remains of our last (we hope) snow storm of the winter are still hanging around under the north sides of our walls and deep in the woods. It was a bad storm for April, and even the old Vermonters picking up their mail in the post office had to search their memories to recall that much snow this late in the year. "April is the cruelest month," as T.S. Eliot wrote. Yup.

Last fall, the *Farmer's Almanac* predicted an unusually snowy winter. I'm so pleased it was correct. Weather forecasting, like everything else these days, has gotten so high-tech ~ satellite maps with amoeba-like blotches of lime green and shocking pink jerking their way from left to right across the screen. It's accurate, it's informative, it's up-to-the-minute, but it's a far cry from the neighboring farmer of my youth: when he wanted to see if the soil had warmed up enough for spring planting, he discreetly lowered his pants and sat on it. No high-tech thermoprobe for him. And he never planted too early.

Each technological advance pushes us one step further away from direct contact with nature. The sailor who feels the weather on his cheeks, like the farmer feeling it on his (although different ones), has an experience that is immediate and direct. When I sit in front of my computer screen watching shapes and colors that bear not the slightest resemblance to weather, my experience is so distanced, so mediated, that it has become, literally, unreal.

I flip an antique table on its back, and I run my fingers over the jack-plane marks under its leaves; I feel a faint, but real, contact between me and the craftsman who made it. We sold a blue and white Delft plate a few months ago. Under its rim was a partial, but perfectly clear, blue fingerprint: the painter had wet paint on her fingers when she picked it up. Every antique has that finger print, even if not so literally. It's the sign of a directness of contact between a man and what he does, between human experience and reality.

The immediacy of this contact between buttock and earth is what we have thrown away in our rush to technologize, televise, and digitize everything. It seems as though we can't have a direct experience of anything anymore ~ all experiences are remote and mediated.

Now don't get me wrong. I'm as high tech as you are, maybe more so. I couldn't function without computers and the internet, without my palm pilot, my cell phone, and my digital camera. They're so efficient, so fast, so precise. In this day and age, technology is the only way to live.

But it's not the only way to live. In our home, the high-tech gadgets are balanced by antiques. Antiques are the products of a low-tech way of life in which people had an immediate contact with reality: their fingerprints were on everything they made, everything they did. They experienced the weather on their cheeks. Antiques give technology a constant reality check.

We need the *Farmer's Almanac* to balance weather.com. My computer is efficient, but my Queen Anne armchair will outlast it. I couldn't live without either, but even more important, I couldn't live with either one of them alone.

ANGEL

I spent a quiet evening recently sitting on the porch with an angel on my lap. I don't know what sort of an angel he actually was – angels are not something I'm very familiar with. He wore a crown, and I've never heard of a crowned angel, but in his hand was a flaming sword, a bit like the ones held by the angels that guarded the gates of Paradise after Adam and Eve were kicked out of it. So I'm going to call him a guardian angel. It sounds good, even if it's not strictly accurate. But his charm to me is that he looks less like an angel, and more like a chubby Elizabethan burgher with wings. Terrestrial, not at all celestial.

He had been carved in oak when Elizabeth I was on the throne, and I was trying to give him that softly glowing patina that I and my customers like. I sat in a low Windsor chair that tipped my lap at just the right angle. Lisa was sitting across the porch from me, her lap completely filled with Cromwell, our huge Maine Coon cat, and a book that she was resting on his back. She'd put soft, mellow jazz on the CD player. Beside my chair, an early joint stool held a glass of red wine at exactly the right height. Spring in Vermont. Bliss before the blackflies.

The carving was intricate with some deep crevices and softly rounded highlights. For much of its life, it had been waxed regularly. Then it must have been owned by someone who was chronically short of time, or who got no pleasure from the look of old waxed wood. The surface had dried and died. No, not died ~ gone into hibernation, it would take only a bit of patience and elbow grease to bring it back to life.

And that's what I was giving it. What was taking my time was the dead wax in the crevices: it had dried to an ugly grayish-white. I had to soften it and take out the excess. It was a slow job, but it was peaceful. It popped into my mind that I would never add the charge for my labor onto the asking price: if I were going to, I'd be tempted to hurry, and that would have been wrong.

Many years ago, I was putting up a fence to replace an old one that had disintegrated. We'd just bought a child's pony, and he was coming the next day, so I was hurrying to get the job finished before nightfall. One of my neighbors, an old hill farmer, whose two collies seemed permanently attached to his ankles, stopped and watched me pound in a stake. It was not quite vertical. "I tell you, John," he said, very gently in his lilting Welsh voice, "twenty years from now, they'll wonder who put that fence up, but they'll never ask how long it took."

It wasn't a rebuke so much as disapproval that I was doing an old-time task in a modern-day manner. It was a verbal antique, a saying crafted in an earlier time that was handed down from Bryn Jones to me, and now from me to you. That's all the provenance I know, but I expect Bryn inherited it from his father, who inherited from his, and so on. It's probably as old as my angel, and it's the reason that my 200-year-old Windsor and my 400-year-old joint stool are still supporting me and my wine glass. They weren't made by men who were desperately charging on to the next project and charging for their labor by the hour. They worked efficiently, yes; but desperately, no.

In an age of rush and hurry, when values are measured in dollars, when every job is pressured by the one that has to be done after it, it's good to be reminded that work can still be done because it's worth doing, not because of what it earns. If a customer happens to ask how long it took to achieve the softly glowing patina that I was able to revive, I'll answer quietly and truthfully, "Oh, about 400 years." You can't charge by the hour for that.

JUNE

SQUARE DANCE

Our downtown was closed and cordoned off last Saturday. Well, downtown is a bit of a grandiose way to refer to our four corners where the General Store, the Community Center, and our tiny green form the core of the village. And we didn't exactly cordon the roads off, we just danced and blocked all the traffic that way.

The locals knew, of course, that this was our annual square dance, and they didn't attempt to drive through. But we sure held up the second homeowners in their SUVs. Dancing really is more important than traffic.

All city folk drive huge SUVs in Vermont so that they are fully equipped for anything that our benign and gentle summers can toss at them. And, as a bonus, they know they'll never get stuck in the little patch of loose gravel outside the store where we all have to pull up to get the paper. Vermonters, by the way, drive Subaru wagons and pick-ups. No exceptions. Period.

Anyway, Luke had pulled up his tractor and trailer upon which Lou, our excellent caller, had set his enormous speakers. And the whole village gathered in groups of eight, where they twirled, held hands, advanced and retreated as Lou called the steps in the falling light. All ages were there, from the toddlers to the totterers, young girls partnered with old men and vice versa. Even Russ, our village constable, joined in, which was just as well, because no one had bothered to find out if we were allowed to block the roads for a summer evening. But then, "I'm a Vermonta, I do what I wanta," as my favorite bumper-sticker puts it.

So the SUVs waited – one of them was a Hummer, now that's really being prepared! No Green Mountain man was going to catch him with his pants down, no sirree!

The dance steps haven't changed in generations, and neither has the way dancers have to join together to enjoy them. Square dancing is as American as apple-pie and blueberries. But it's not American in the way that Big America struts on the world stage. It's Small America, and all the better for it. It's Small America that people seek and find in Vermont.

Square dancing and antiques preserve the long-held values of Small America. They don't get the headlines and camera coverage like the doings of Big America, but that doesn't mean they're any the less important. In fact, if you stop and think about it, it means they're actually more important. They're not newsworthy because they're not new, and they haven't changed since yesterday. They want to pull people together, holding hands in a circle: they don't set people in competition with one another. They're not dangerous or threatening. They don't conflict with anybody or anything. Except perhaps an impatient Hummer.

Small America survives best in small villages and the countryside, which is why people from the suburbs and the skyscrapers and the sweatshops spend as much time here as they possibly can. And it's why, every now and again, a square dance darn well should stop an SUV dead in its tracks.

DINNER

We threw a small dinner party the other night, just two couples and Lisa and I sitting around our old table, a chipped transferware pitcher full of fresh peonies from the garden in the middle. A great evening, a great mix of the old and the new.

One couple was a pair of old, dear friends, the other new friends. The new ones have just moved into the village, where they are, I'm sure, going to be widely welcomed. Twenty-five years ago, they escaped from Poland, and after a harrowing journey during which they were separated and reunited, when they never knew if one stage would be their last, they finally got here with no money, no possessions, no English, and no history. They had left everything except their bodies and their determination behind them.

And now they have, as we say, made it. Fluent in English, a prosperous business, and a nice new house full of new things. They were very interested in our antiques, they enjoyed eating at a 350-year-old table, and they loved my killer syllabub – an eighteenth-century dessert that is basically oodles of heavy cream laced with Madeira, lemon juice, sugar, and cinnamon. We served it in period glasses and ate it with period spoons. Delicious, but don't even think of your arteries!

Antiques interested them, but didn't speak to them. For them, the past was something to be left behind, not lived with in the present. America is the land of the new and the future. And they love America – they love America with the personal passion of those who have lived in a society that was so, so different. In the Poland that they left, everything was old, and shabby, and worn out. There was nothing new, there was nothing that worked well. They lived with old things, repaired them and re-used them, not because they wanted to, or because they loved them, but because they had to.

They had no history. The communist regime had wiped out all traces of the Poland that used to be, it was off the curriculum in schools, it was never talked about or written about, and any traces that remained were overlaid with the official meaning that they were the bad old days, the days of inequality, poverty, and bondage. You have no identity when you have no history, and that of course, is precisely what the regime wanted ~ a society of people without identity.

Talking with them made me feel deeply privileged to have lived my life in countries with histories – England and America. Both nations have histories that deserve to be kept alive, even if we're not proud of everything that happened in them. And both of these deeply historical societies have always been great innovators, both have consistently pushed modernity forward, both have been the engines of historical change.

Those are the sort of societies that produce antiques and the people who love them. You can't have antiques if you're not constantly moving forward. Every antique goes through a similar lifecycle: first it is new and in fashion; then it is old fashioned, neglected, and inert; and, then finally, it is reborn into something beautiful, revered, and cherished – an antique. It's a caterpillar-chrysalis-butterfly cycle. Communist Poland was held fast in the chrysalis stage.

I know that our new friends loved eating an eighteenth-century dessert out of eighteenth-century glasses with eighteenth-century spoons. But that sort of history-in-the-present was the sort that had been eradicated from their lives. Early in the twentieth century, when the value of antiques was becoming widely recognized, many museums created series of period rooms that were explicitly intended to give immigrants a historical dimension to their new identities as Americans. It was a great idea, but I think an oversimplified one. You can't give someone a new history, you can't replace one history with another. There are many different ways of being American, and living with antiques is only one of them. You can live in the America of the now and the future, and you can create your own history while you are doing so. That, after all, is the way that a nation of immigrants constantly reinvents itself.

Around that table were multi-generation Americans, brand new first-generation Americans, and me, a first-generation American with a similar history to the old Americans. Our home, too, is furnished with American and English antiques, as well as with brand new American things. That evening, our friends and our furnishings matched each other – surely, that's the way it should be.

JULY

PARADE

Our Fourth of July Parade doesn't change much. There's the fire truck. We don't have a high school, so we won't have a marching band, but there'll be the fire truck. We're too small for the politicians, so we do without their plastic grins from open air cars, courtesy of the local dealership (which we don't have, either). But we have a fire truck. We don't have a VFW Post, but we do have veterans, and they'll be there. We don't have elaborate floats, but we all have lawn tractors, and they'll be there, decked out in variations of red-white-and-blue (aren't we lucky that our flag has such cheerful colors, just right for a bright July day.) And we have kids, and they'll be there, in fancy dress and face paint (why do kids love painting their faces, is it because paint is a sort of permissible dirt?).

But we do have one huge problem. How do we divide ourselves up between marchers and watchers? If all the kids are in the parade, who's going to get out of control on the sidewalks? Not that we have sidewalks, but you know what I mean. You big-city folks may be worried about all your urban problems, but I want you to know that life up here in the hills is pretty complicated too.

Then there'll be a barbecue, and games by the lake, and we'll have raked up the goose-poop -- Canadians get us cheap prescription drugs for our old folks, so I suppose we should put up with their doggoned geese. And of course, there'll be flags, flags everywhere.

It'll be a great day, and, I predict, someone, on hearing my English accent, will ask how we celebrate July Fourth over there. Now, modest and self-deprecating as we Brits are, not even we celebrate the most humiliating defeat in our history! Sometimes, when mischief gets the better of tact, I hear myself replying, "It's great, but we call it "Good Riddance Day!'" But what the heck, lose a colony, gain a friend – that's OK by me.

Actually, the question is much more reasonable than my poking fun at it might suggest. There's not the slightest trace of anti-Englishness in the celebrations. The flags flying everywhere carry no hint that their original was flown against the English. Now, they are merely positive, they signify what they stand for, not what they stood against. And I'm glad that people assume that the English would celebrate as well. July Fourth is a time for all-inclusive, welcoming celebrations. (I suppose the fact that the day is more often called the Fourth of July than Independence Day is another sign that its history of conflict has dropped away, and it is now a day to experience patriotism as a unifying emotion.)

And that makes me wonder whether we antique lovers shouldn't fly reproductions of our original flag among all the contemporary ones, or better yet, reproductions of the many forms that the flag has taken. The Stars and Stripes is unique: it is the only national flag that has changed and grown as the nation has changed and grown. Reminding ourselves of what the flag looked like at different stages of our history reminds us that we are a nation that has constantly struggled toward unity, that the flag stands for a meaning of America that all our forebears worked for, that we all share today, and that we can all look up to.

Like all antiques, antique flags bring with them the positive side of our history: they link us to the past that has been productive. All history is selective. The history embedded in our antiques is the one we are proud of, and the one we can take forward into the future with us. It's not the history of divisive politics, but the history of the consensus that we've achieved out of those arguments. Antiques are above politics.

We degrade our flag when we taint it with politics, and sadly, today, the flag can be dragged down into that divisive arena. But not on the Fourth of July, and certainly not up here in the Green Mountains. Our flags fly higher than contentious versions of patriotism. We paint the flag on our kids' faces – and there's no better way of flying the flag than that.

INDEPENDENCE

Each Memorial Day, we do a show at the Brandywine River Museum in Chadds Ford, Pennsylvania, and all around us, the flags are flying. Probably many will stay on the lamp posts until the Fourth of July.

This year, the Museum had mounted an exhibition of English pottery to coincide with the show. The pottery had been made for the American market and was exported between 1780 and 1820, just when the American struggle for independence was at its height, and in whose early days, half a mile down the road, George Washington was temporarily defeated by General Howe at the battle of Brandywine.

It was a period when, understandably, anti-Englishness was at its peak. Many an American household showed its patriotism by boycotting tea, whose tax had come to stand for the unfairness and selfishness of English colonialism. Yet the exhibit contained many teapots. It also contained pitchers made in England but decorated with portraits of Washington and with engravings of the American ships that fought the English.

Now of course, English manufacturers were desperately trying to hang onto their biggest market, even in wartime. They were happy sell to the "enemy" and to decorate their wares with enemy symbols if that's what they had to do to keep the money flowing. But that doesn't explain, at least not adequately, why American consumers kept buying from the enemy. The utility factor, of course, explains some of it. Americans needed plates and pitchers and pots, and English pottery was the best bargain: it was all there was that was both available and affordable.

But I don't think that utility explains all that was going on. I think beauty had something to do with it as well. Beauty doesn't recognize national borders, it pays no attention to politicians' definitions of what makes one nationality different from another. A ship or a portrait beautifully painted in England on a pot to be sold in America remains beautiful whether there's a war on or not. The English woman who painted it and the American woman who bought it were sharing something that was deeper by far than the divisive politics of their day. Beauty unites human beings, politics divides them.

It was the beauty of the pottery that was exhibited at the Brandywine River Museum, not its politics. Beauty lasts, politics, thank heaven, do not. In my ideal world, all politicians would be steeped in art history. On every foreign trip, they would spend at least as much time in museums and art galleries as in conference rooms. And when politicians of other nations visited us, we would take them to the National Gallery before the White House. And, of course, all politicians would collect antiques! Dream on!

Art and antiques are there to remind us that while we are Americans, or English, or whatever, we are also human beings, and that what makes us human lies deeper than what makes us American or English. I feel comfortable being American-and-English, my (wonderful) marriage is American-and-English, I sell English antiques to American collectors who put them in American houses and live with them as Americans. At our front door, on Independence Day, we will fly the Union Jack alongside the Stars and Stripes. Independence does not mean separateness: it's a point from which to connect, not divide.

JUST US

High summer in Vermont. Last Saturday was our town's Mount Holly Day (we're proud of that pun.) It's when we have fun down by the lake, nothing fancy, just us. The summer folk are here, and they joined in with the year-rounders and the old Vermonters: all of us together. Games for the kids ~ the only rule was that the one who screamed loudest won. Adults had games too: Lisa won the mixed doubles in the canoe races, not with me, I hasten to explain, but with Chris, who helps us load and unload our van: a wise choice on her part.

And of course, there was the ever-popular Doo-Doo Drop. For a week before there'd been a chart of squares, 20 by 20, on the counter at the store. You bought a square and wrote your name in it. On Saturday, on the far side of the games area, Luke had fenced a square, 20 yards by 20 yards. At the height of the fun, he brought his quiet old Holstein and shooed her inside. We all stopped, and crowded around watching breathlessly till she lifted her tail and picked the winner. The proceeds all went to the Community

Association, and all the burgers, salads and pies were free if you were a member. If you weren't, you joined on the spot, or you went hungry. Just us.

Well, the geese were there, too. They'd moved in from Canada a couple of years ago, and if you know geese, you know the raking we had to do before the games could get started. And there's Eurasian milfoil in the lake, we've managed to keep the swimming area clear, but over the rest of the lake, the milfoil's doing better than we are. But we can cope with these aliens. It was still just us.

Jeb and his band were under our tent (the one that normally shelters us at outdoor antiques shows). When he's not making music, Jeb's our stonemason and landscape gardener. Tracy, the rhythm guitar, does something with computers for the state way down there in Rutland, and the others do whatever they have to to make a living in Vermont.

Jeb and his band played for us again on Wednesday evening. Our town green is tiny. Not particularly picturesque, it climbs up the hill with a couple of Scots pines and some maples to give it shade. The band was under the pines on the flatter bit at the bottom: the rest of us sat above them on lawn chairs, blankets, or just the grassy bank. We were all there, from the toddlers who could hardly walk, to the seniors who could hardly toddle.

The music was folksy, bluesy, tuneful, just what we wanted. Then Jeb swung into "Sue's Subaru." Tracy's wife Sue used to drive an ancient Volvo that wouldn't start in the cold and got stuck in two inches of snow. There's not an able-bodied person among us who hasn't given that old Volvo a jump start, or a push, or both. Now, she's got a Subaru. Next winter won't be the same ~ we can hardly wait. We made the maples quiver as we joined in the chorus celebrating "Sue's Subaru." "Milfoil Blues," another of Jeb's originals, was pretty popular, too. No prize for guessing why.

But the high spot came with The Apples ~ Jeb's daughter Jenny, Tracey's step-daughter Anna-Lisa, and their friend. Gangly ten- and twelve year-olds, all long and thin ~ arms, legs and hair ~ with smiles that split their faces. Jenny had written a song about her dog Beau: she sang the lead, while her friends harmonized on the other mike and did the doo-wops. Anna-Lisa found that she could harmonize best with her back to the audience, but Jenny stood four-square, grasping the mike stand with both hands. And her voice filled the sky.

Our heart-strings were tugged almost as hard by the final number. Jeb led us all in Woody Guthrie's "This Land Is My Land." Even the Scots pines shook this time. And when we finished ~ we all stood up and we sang it again.

Yep, geese, milfoil, terrorists ~ they're all from out there, and we're here. Just us. And we're staying here. And we'll sing "this land belongs to you and me" just as often as we durn well like.

SMALL ADULTS

One of the many good things about living in a village that's a bit out of step with the rest of the country is the way we mix generations together. There simply aren't enough of us to form separate age-groups. Even our teenagers, occasionally at least, mix in public with adults and young kids. Wow!

I don't know many kids: to tell the truth (whisper it very quietly), I don't like them very much: the best thing my own children ever did was to grow up. So obviously, I'm no child psychologist, I'm just an old grouch with too many years under his belt, but I get the distinct impression that it's a hard life being a kid in twenty-first-century America. Perhaps part of the problem is that we've made childhood so special that we've unwittingly turned our kids into aliens whom we don't understand and who are best kept at a distance. "If you dine with the devil, use a long spoon," as my grandmother used to say.

It wasn't always like that. In fact, there was a time when childhood was ordinary, not special. A few weeks ago we sold a child's chest that had been made in seventeenth-century England. It was a beauty, and I love to think of the little girl kneeling in front of it 400 years ago, rummaging for her dolls or her bonnet or whatever treasures she had stowed inside. I bet she traced her fingers around the carving and made different patterns out of it. The chest was small, not just because she was, but because she had very few toys or personal possessions. The idea that kids need lots of things to be kids is a modern phenomenon.

So her chest was nothing like a piece of modern children's furniture. It was made and decorated just like an adult's. It was smaller, that was the only difference. Ordinary, not special. It was not made of garish plastic decorated with distorted cartoon figures. Children had highchairs then as well as today. And their chairs were carved and decorated just like adult chairs. The same, but smaller. There was no idea that children's things had to belong to a different world with a different aesthetic than adults' things. Quite the opposite, in fact. Her mother saw her daughter as an adult-in-the-making, not as a separate genus of the human species.

SMALL ADULTS

Seventeenth-century children were miniature adults. Look at children's portraits from the period and notice how adult their expressions look: no cuteness or coyness there. Our ancestors saw a smooth continuity between childhood and adulthood, we've separated them.

Now, I'm not saying that the seventeenth-century way of being a child was better or worse than ours. What I am saying is that it was different. There is no evidence that their children were more or less happy than ours. There is no evidence that they grew up to become more or less well adjusted adults. They just grew up differently.

An antique that can stimulate us to imagine that sort of difference enriches our lives. A society without antiques can all too easily become complacently comfortable in its assumption that its own way of living is the only way, and it never is. If the American imagination were limited to contemporary American culture, we would be creatively impoverished and headed for decadence. Oh dear, perhaps we are.

And that's quite a lesson for a child to teach us.

SEPTEMBER

THE REAL US

The fall is our busy period up here in Vermont. Our winding roads are full of blue-plate specials (blue license plates from Connecticut), yellow perils (from New Jersey), and the black-and-whites from New York. The drivers have their eyes on the hills not the road, and they drive so slowly they even make an old timer in his old time pick-up impatient. Leaf-peepers are drivers from hell, their speed has nothing to do with road conditions, they're prone to stop on the sharpest curve and leap out with a camera leaving the door open and the engine running. They wouldn't do that in the suburbs. But we can't keep our beauty to ourselves: they have a right to share it. We're privileged to live in a place that gives so much pleasure to so many out-of-staters.

Ever since the early 1800s Americans have migrated to the cities and suburbs, but their hearts have remained in the countryside. Rural New England may be on the margins of the economic and political life of the nation, but symbolically we're central. America is an urbanized society, but in the hearts of most Americans, the real America is rural.

The same sort of contradiction holds true for antiques. America is the most modern and future-oriented nation in the world, but it's deeply traditional. We live in the present and we work for the future, but our hearts are in the past. And that's a lot of the reason that it is so enjoyable to go antiquing in New England in the fall. New England is such a good match for peoples' sense of what America really is, but modern America actually isn't. The landscapes and small towns are still traditional and rural – and from their barns and attics the antiques still emerge to remind us of who we wish to think we are. The summer and fall antiques shows and the shops that put on special seasonal displays are all, in their way, giving back to Americans the part of their identity that they can't find in the leafy suburbs and grid-locked cities. Antiques are material nostalgia.

In the real world, the first part of the twenty-first century has been lousy. The economy has kicked us in the pants so hard and so often that we can no longer bear to sit down to read about it, the rest of the world appears to be full of people who hate us, and everywhere that we thought was safe and trustworthy has us looking over our shoulders in suspicion or fear. But in our hearts we know our country is not really like that. The media's endless tales of gloom and doom paint a picture whose surface seems utterly realistic, but underneath, we just know that it's not like that, it really isn't.

The material nostalgia of an antique is actually more truthful than the factual reports on the nightly news. The sense of self-recognition that city-dwellers experience on the winding roads of Vermont is no illusion, it is no nostalgia falsely shaped by wish-fulfillment. It's an experience of what the poet called "the-once-and-always-will-be."

There's more truth in an antique than in a newspaper headline. A Vermont country store is more real than security checks at airports. The men who made the antiques we live with are more American than the men who made Enron. And that's why we need antiques.

CIDER DAYS

Up here in the Green Mountains, we mark the change from fall to winter by celebrating Cider Days. The village has an old cider press that Jim, its custodian, tows onto the green every second weekend in October. Local orchards donate apples by the bushel, we fire up the ancient motor, and we take it in turns to tip the apples into the hopper at the top and fill the jugs at the bottom.

We get a good crowd. They come for the craft and art stalls around the edge of the Green, they come to buy fresh-pressed cider (nothing like it!), but mostly they come to stand around and gossip. Gossip turns a village into a community, and events like Cider Days don't just make money for the Community Association, but the association of people builds the community.

There are more red leaves on the grass than on the trees. The kids shuffle through them. And even though it's sunny, the winter coats are out, and if you're

very observant, you might spot a pair of gloves – the
first sighting of the season.

    Of course, the Community Historical Museum
is open, fifty yards from the Green, just below the store
and post office, in case you're looking for it, across
the street from our all-volunteer library. It's a low-key,
slightly dusty museum in what was once a blacksmith's
shop. It's full of the antiques of everyday life – niddy-
noddies, old dolls, kitchen baskets, and, of course,
brown photographs – the sort of antiques you'll find in
many a Vermont summer antique show. But here, each
antique is carefully labeled with the name of the family
who used it and the name of the villager who gave it.
It's the names that matter. We know whose hands put
the patina on the little wooden ladle. Those hands lived
in our village, and that ladle will stay in our village.

    In an antique show or shop, antiques are
individual items for sale: in the museum, they're the
living past of our community, which is why we look at
the labels more closely than we look at the antiques.
This little doll's chair isn't just any old doll's chair: it
was made in the toy factory that, just over a hundred
years ago, was our village's largest employer. Its red and
yellow paint came from the ochre mine two villages

away down in the valley. Its wood was felled on our hillsides. The man who made it lived in our village. And so did the girl who played with it. And so does her granddaughter who donated it.

We live with our past, but not in it. And we look to the future as well. We want our past to shape that future, not commercial pressures, not rootless outsiders with fat checkbooks. If we can shape our future, we'll keep the continuity that makes a community. And that's what we've been trying to do.

On Cider Days this year, we celebrated the success of our first-ever land conservation project. Hundreds of people came together to conserve 120 acres of farm- and woodland. Now, it can never be built on: the fields will always be farmed; the woods will always be open to our children, they will never be fenced and posted. Our grandchildren will enjoy those meadows with the wooded hillside rising behind them. Just as we do today. And just as did the settlers who built our little community in those hard, hard times that we like to think about, but probably couldn't have survived in.

If only we allowed our antiques, and the people who made and used them, more influence in shaping our present and our future, I can't help thinking that our country, and the world, would be a better place.

DARKNESS

Friends visited us from Manhattan a couple of weekends ago. They'd rented a car (not owning one shows how seriously Manhattan they were) and they'd left in plenty of time to drive all but the last hour or so in daylight. The phone call came just as the final, yellowish light of day was silhouetting the ridge of the mountains across from our house. They'd reached Bennington, just an hour away, and they'd be with us in good time for a glass of wine before dinner.

The hour came, but they didn't. An hour and a half, and still no sign of them. No phone call either, they were in deep Vermont with no cell coverage. We stopped being polite hosts and poured ourselves a glass each. Finally, just shy of two hours later, headlights turned uncertainly into our driveway. We threw on coats and went out to greet them. They slumped, exhausted, in the front seats. "Phew," he sighed, "It's so dark!" "And then," she chipped in, "there were all those signs warning of moose!"

We were sympathetic, we really were. We honestly didn't even chuckle at the thought of New

Yorkers, who had probably never driven in the dark before, crawling along our twisty Vermont roads, their eyes straining through the windshields, and their bodies quivering with terror at the thought of all those monstrous moose threatening to leap out at them from the woods on either side.

Not only had our friends never driven in the dark, they'd hardly ever seen it. They climbed shakily out of the car and looked upward. It was one of those autumnal nights in Vermont, cold, still, and crystal clear. The Milky Way was like a solid, silvery-grey ribbon, and the rest of the sky was peppered with stars of every size and brightness. There was no moon, but we didn't need it: we could see clearly across the meadow to the black sides of the mountain and up to the ridge, sharp against the dark blue of the sky. Their jaws dropped: "Wow!" was all they could say.

Indoors, we relaxed around the woodstove. As we talked we realized that most Americans never see dark, not real dark, and so few, so rarely, see a sky bright with stars. We couldn't help wondering how well our friends would sleep – there is deep, heavy silence all around us at night. Literally not a sound for hours. That's as rare as the dark for most people.

But it never used to be. Silence and dark and stars were normal experiences, at least they were before all those cities grew up and sucked people into their de-natured ways of living. The communities where stars and dark and silence were part of life were also the communities that made their own furniture and snowshoes and houses.

Our friends are delightful people, but they don't understand the appeal of antiques. I have to wonder if never experiencing the dark and never experiencing antiques aren't actually two sides of the same loss. That loss is something most Americans live with without knowing it. For them, night is when the streetlights come on. For them, the past is an alien country, full of the unknown, like those ferocious moose, and they have no wish to revisit it. The past is as alien to the present as the dark is to the streetlight as the country is to the city. That's their loss.

So I feel a sort of mission to show people that the past is good, that the present is better when connected to the past, and that antiques and dark and silence are good for the soul. After all, Manhattanites still have souls, and even their souls need nourishment.

KITCHEN

On my hands and knees searching for my coffee mug among the dishes in the bathtub, I found myself pondering the problem of blending the new with the old. You see, Lisa is having her kitchen done. After years of saving her pennies, she decided that the pile was now big enough and she could go ahead. So ahead she went. And wow! What a pile of pennies you need to do a kitchen these days! It's a good thing that we have a truck, otherwise I'd never have gotten them to the bank.

The consequence is that we have no water on the first floor (somehow the first floor bathroom managed to get itself involved in the remodeling). Hence the dishes in the bathtub, and hence, also, the problem of the-new-with-the-old.

We live in a nineteenth-century Vermont farmhouse, so Lisa didn't want cabinets with synthetic surfaces, however easy they may be to clean. There's nothing shiny in the whole house, so she didn't want lacquered cherry. So we're having a painted surface in a traditional color. Our designer/supplier asked if we wanted the cabinets aged ~ "distressed" is the word she actually used. That would have distressed us far more than the cabinets. As antique dealers we are hypersensitive about artificially aged surfaces: they scream "Wrong!!" They telegraph the fakery underneath them. So no distress for the cabinets or us.

The cabinets will look traditional, but new, which is what they are. And are they new! Their insides unfold, spin around, do somersaults and one will even hand you the salt if you ask it nicely. The appliances are all stainless steel ~ blatantly new because there is no traditional look to fit them into.

In the middle of the room, we'll put our antique farmhouse table whose top is genuinely "distressed" ~ what a stupid word that is: the marks that two hundred years of cooks have left upon it are imaginatively enriching, not distressing. Around it will be a set of Windsor chairs that we are just beginning to assemble, one by one. And I know we'll find room for a few antique accessories, such as a spice cabinet or a small set of hanging shelves.

Lisa is pretty confident that it is all going to "work," as designers say: I must admit to being more concerned that it will "work" for the chef. Lisa cooks like an angel, lucky me.

We enjoy living with antiques, but we have to mix the new with the old in some fashion. We want the efficiency and comforts of modern life, but we also want our antiques to soften the edginess of modernity and to give it that sense of human history that it chillingly lacks.

Some are very purist about the way they live with antiques. They want to be able to step into a mini-world of the past that shuts the present day out. I have spent many happy evenings with friends whose rooms are furnished entirely in period (with the exception in every case of electric lights). Sipping wine out of hand-blown glasses in a period room really does give one the sense of time-travel: there's a completeness to the experience that a modern coffee table, for instance, would shatter. And you know, it's easier to hold a real conversation in a room like this, with no TV, no background music, no telephone, and not a remote control in sight. Talking with family and neighbors was our forebears' main leisure activity, and period furnishings encourage period behavior.

There's no formula telling us how to live with antiques. In our case, our dining room is fairly purist, our living room much more eclectic. We each of us have to find our own way, the one that works for us. But luckily (and let's pat ourselves on the back a little) the desire to live with antiques is the mark of a creative imagination that does not want to follow the fashion of the day, that does not want to create an interior that resembles everyone else's. Antiques have individual personalities, and so do those who choose to live with them. Sheep don't collect antiques.

We should thank our stars that antiques bring a different dimension to a society in which the market-driven pressures to dress alike, behave alike, and think alike are so pervasive and so powerful. Hey, let your rebellious streak come out ~ collect antiques!

Oh, and while you're at it, please help me find my coffee mug in the bath tub.

NOVEMBER

SAYINGS

It's November, the quiet, grey time in Vermont. The leaf-peepers have gone home, the skiers and the second-home owners have stayed on the flatlands, and we have Vermont to ourselves. But we don't like it very much. November shouldn't happen in Vermont. Vermont's colors are white, blue, green, and, of course, in the fall, red. November is grey, unrelenting grey.

Mick farms the land across the road from us. He's close to seventy, and his son, Art, and nephew, Dave, do most of the work. (I'll need help if Mick ever reads this!) But Mick can stay on the tractor for hour after hour. He told me, with a glint of pride in his eyes, about a farmer friend who's only a few years older than he: "It's surprising," his friend complained, "that I seem to have done my full day's work by ten o'clock in the morning." Next year will see the family's hundredth anniversary on the same farm. That doesn't happen too often, these days. Vermont farming is in bad shape. So are Mick's knees. But his spirit's as spry as the day he was born.

He was brush-hogging the edges of the hay meadows on a grey November morning. He stopped the tractor and leant down to talk to me about the weather. There's a lot of weather to talk about in Vermont, so that's what we do. His mother, he remembered, used to say of November:

> No sun, no moon,
> No night, no noon,
> Nor any time of day.

I love the wisdom of country life. Sayings like this are verbal antiques: they are something made in the past that is alive in the present. There's a countryman's rhythm in the words that's as valid today as it was a hundred years ago. This one has stuck in my mind: any heavy sky will trigger it. Today, when we want to know the time, we look down at our wrist, not up at the sky.

When Mick's mother was young, time was something you went with, and fitted your life into. Now time doesn't organize us, we organize it. The wristwatch, not the sun, determines the pattern of our day. Our diaries are where we organize our days, not where we record what we did in them. We're so much more efficient.

I had the same mixed feelings as I was lighting the woodstove. I struck the match, put it to the paper, shut the door, and the job was done. The day before, I'd hung my nose over, and very nearly bought, a tin candleholder whose base was a tinderbox made to contain a striker and tinder. Striking a spark, nurturing it in the tinder, and transferring the flame to where you wanted it was a domestic art that required a steady hand, patience, and, of course, time. The first strike rarely caught. It was inefficient.

Notice that with our highly efficient box of matches, we still use the same word – "strike" – even though what we do is scrape. Scraping a match is so much more predictable, quicker, and less skillful than striking a light. But, just stop for a moment, and say those two phrases aloud. Which one touches your imagination and draws you to it? And which one puts you off? If we're antique lovers, our modern efficiency gives us mixed feelings: the inefficiency that it replaces always had other qualities whose passing causes regret. The regret for what inevitably had to go is what we call nostalgia.

An antique has an aura of nostalgia, a second-hand object doesn't. Nostalgia makes an antique antique. Nostalgia reminds us that progress involves loss as well as gain. Living with antiques enables us to enjoy the gains of progress while reducing its losses. Nostalgia often gets a bad rap in these hard-headed days: people think it makes the past too sweet and sentimental. Of course it does, but all memories are selective, and there's nothing wrong with recalling the good bits, and tucking them in the back of our minds as we live our lives in the modern way. Mick was on a huge, modern, throbbing tractor when he remembered his mother's saying about November.

No night, no noon, no sun, no moon, nor any time of day. I'm glad I've got a wristwatch, and a box of matches ~ and yet ... I should go back and see if that tinderbox-candleholder is still for sale. It'd be good to have a steel striker and flint to remind me of the past.

But I'll still scrape a match to light the stove.

CLEARING

Up here in Vermont, our first snow has often come and gone by November. Today, I was getting ready for it. It was a glorious late-fall day, blue cloudless sky, leaves like copper and brass, and silence as deep as the woods where I was working. Well, working is hardly the word. I had my long-handled loppers and a small bow saw, and I was leisurely working my way along one of the old farm roads that wind their way through our woods. There are old stone walls running aimlessly through them as well, signs that the woodland, now thick with maple, birch, and cherry, was once open farmland, probably only two or three generations ago.

Sheep and cattle, I expect. Now, it's tired, stressed humans who wander through the woods seeking a different form of sustenance. So do deer and moose, and bears and foxes, I see all their tracks alongside the industrial patterns left by my boots. Soon, it'll be skis and snowshoes.

That's why I'm here. I'm lopping off the small branches that hang down over the road and the saplings that are starting to grow up through it. I have to reach up high, because a branch that's way over my head as I walk along the road in the fall will be right in Lisa's face when she skis along it in winter. A coating of snow does that to young branches.

I was enjoying the break from my computer and my can of wax polish. I was happy to be out there, keeping an old road open and helping to preserve the traces of a life that's gone, though not completely. The road is no longer for horses and wagons. It's for skiers and walkers, and, occasionally, for Jack's grandkids on their snowmobiles. I hate snowmobiles, they're noisy and smelly, and their speed desecrates the forest. But I like Jack, he's a neighbor, and a good one, and most times being neighborly is more important than having opinions.

I knew that the joint stool we'd just acquired was waiting for me indoors. It needed another waxing. It's starting to regain the patina it had lost through benign neglect, the patina that brings out its age and beauty. Would a coat of wax do the same for me, I wonder? I guess not, I'm no antique – there's no way I'm getting more beautiful as I get older. Oh well.

I've wandered off my point. The joint stool will eventually become somebody's end table: nobody will ever sit on it at the dinner table as its original owner did. Things last, but what we use them for may change. No matter, their history remains in their new use. A bit like that old farm road in the woods; no horse will ever again pull a wagon of hay along it. But it will still play its role in human life, just a different role in a different life. Times change, but things don't, not if we look after them.

PING PONG

Vermont has turned beautiful again. The first storm of the winter was late, but it's arrived, and it's covering November's brown landscape with the white that we love. It's early snow, so it's the heavy sort, not the sparkling powder we get in February. But it's here in time for Christmas.

Our friend John has had a tough time recently, and has just come home after abdominal surgery. Not surprisingly, this has slowed him down somewhat, and to help out, we went down to Rutland to pick up a ping pong table he's giving his son for Christmas. Ping pong table? That thing was built to Olympic specifications, and if ever we get an earthquake, we'll all know where to shelter! It weighed 300 pounds and was folded into a mattress-shaped box with nowhere to grip. Three college football players loaded it from the Sears pick-up door into our van, but there was no way a guy with his gut held together with staples and a grey-bearded antique dealer with a wonky hip was going to unload that thing and get it down the basement steps.

So we called for reinforcements (Sears' parking lot is one of the very few places in central Vermont where a cell phone actually works.) John organized a couple of strong friends to meet us. The big, wet snowflakes were falling steadily, and the light was fading to that deep grey of a snow storm at dusk as we crawled up John's steep driveway. His driveway winds upward for quarter of a mile through pine woods until it reaches a stand of hundred-year old maples, where it swings sharp right to climb the final slope to the house.

It was here that Bill, one of the reinforcements, was stuck. He was in a front-wheel drive tin can that should never be allowed on dirt roads in the snow, and he was a flatlander. Of course he got stuck. Pulled up behind him was John, who had been running last minute errands in his truck. Just after I stopped behind him to find out what was up, Kyle, the second reinforcement, pulled up behind me. There was no way Bill's tin can was going to move upward: every time we tried to push it, the front wheels slid sideways, closer to the ditch. So a convoy of four vehicles had to inch slowly backward through the woods in the now pitch dark, down a narrow, slushy, twisty driveway, with wet snow blocking our rear windows and exterior mirrors.

Wow, were we intrepid! Now ladies, you have to realize that we guys need to feel intrepid every now and again, especially if we can do so in a warm van listening to VPR. There's nothing like intrepidity in comfort to put a guy in touch with the real man inside.

Vermont's weather can cause problems for antique furniture as well. An eighteenth-century center table that we had brought over from England has just popped open ~ the gap between the two boards of its top has widened a tad as it adjusted to our funny climate. It'll be easy to tighten it up again, and at least we know that it's done what it has to in order to adapt to Vermont. I can sympathize with it: as an Englishman myself, I've had to cope with exactly the same change. But I didn't come apart at the seams, I just became intrepid.

FEASTING

When Elizabeth I was ruling England, Thomas Tusser wrote the first advice book on running a household. He called it Five Hundred Points of Good Husbandry, and in Chapter 10, The Farmer's Daily Diet, he wrote,

> At Christmas play and make good cheer,
> For Christmas comes but once a year.

Now that we've reminded ourselves where that saying comes from, let's take a look at what he's talking about.

A feast in Medieval England would have made our groaning Christmas table look like a soup kitchen. In 1251, for example, Henry III gave a modest wedding banquet for his daughter. He served the guests 1,300 deer, 7,000 hens, 170 boars, 60,000 herring, and 68,500 loaves of bread. I guess that caused a few girdles to be loosened. Admittedly, it was a sign of wealth and power to serve more than could possibly be eaten, and a worthwhile act of charity to give the plentiful leftovers to the poor. But even then ...

We're wrong to think of our forebears as crude, caring only about the quantity they could eat. Their palates were as sophisticated as ours, and their chefs every bit as skillful. They liked thick, strong, spicy sauces in particular. Mawmeny, for instance, was a popular dish consisting of ground meat (beef, pork, or mutton) that was boiled in red wine and covered in a rich sauce that had a wine base thickened by chicken and almonds pounded to a pulp in a mortar and pestle, and then flavored with cloves, sugar, and fried almonds.

Every chef used generous quantities of ginger, mace, cloves, cumin, cardamom, cinnamon, honey, and vinegar, as well as the basics of salt, pepper, and sugar. But strong and complex tastes weren't enough. Medieval diners wanted their food to stimulate their eyes as much as their palates. They dyed their mawmeny either bright red or blue (personally, I'd go for the red -- I wonder why blue food seems such an alien concept to us). Food dyes were made from sandalwood (red), indigo (blue), saffron (yellow), mint or parsley juice (green), and burnt bread crumbs (black).

Chefs were not only visual artists, they were ingenious engineers as well. They would take a peacock, for instance, skin it carefully, and then re-fill it with the cooked meat so that they could present the bird in its full, magnificent plumage. Try that with your turkey. Often, they filled larger animals with smaller ones, like edible Russian dolls. They'd stuff a blackbird stuffed with pinenuts and sugar into a rooster into a pig. Or they'd cut a pike into three, boil the head, fry the body, roast the tail, and then re-assemble the fish for serving (for some reason, this dish was called "glazed pilgrim").

There was none of our parsimonious habit of serving only one main dish per course (that custom began in the nineteenth century): each course of a three-course dinner consisted of multiple dishes of meat, bird, fish, and fruit, sometimes as many as fifteen. All were served at the same time, a bit like a Chinese meal today. Every course finished with a "subtlety," an elaborate structure of marzipan modeled into shapes that flattered the host or the most important guest. At the enthronement of Archbishop Warham at Canterbury in 1504, one of the "subtilties" depicted "Sainte Eustace kneelynge in a Parke under a great tree ful of roses, and a white harte before hym with a crucifyx betweene his hornes, and a man by him leadynge his horse." A medieval feast was a thing of beauty, an enormous thing of beauty, maybe, but a thing of beauty nonetheless. It pleased the eye as much as it strained the belly.

"Eat, drink, and be merry" is a motto with a long, long history. To make us truly merry, a meal should please as many senses as possible. Early cooks knew as well as we do that a really pleasurable meal should be presented beautifully as well as cooked deliciously. Medieval diners also knew, perhaps better than us, that it is impossible to be both merry and moderate – that's an oxymoron. Christmas comes but once a year, so let's indulge in the way that our forebears did, without guilt, anxiety, or any thought of the bathroom scales. May no tightening belts reduce our appetites. Let's eat well at Christmas, and wisely in the New Year.

ABOUT THE AUTHOR

John Fiske was born in Bristol, England, and raised in the Cotswolds before emigrating first to Australia and then to the United States. He is Professor Emeritus of Communication Arts at the University of Wisconsin and is Editor-in-Chief of the *New England Antiques Journal*. He and his wife, Lisa Freeman, are antique dealers specializing in seventeenth-century English oak furniture.

ABOUT THE ARTIST

Robert Sydorowich paints the Vermont countryside, where he has lived for over forty years. He studied art and architecture at the Pratt Institute and the New School for Social Research in New York City.

East Corinth (April)

Suzy (November)

Concert (August)

Sap Buckets (March)

Hay Bales (September)

Ascutney (January)

Grist Mill (February)

Long Trail (October)

Spring Flowers (May)

Christmas (December)

Bethel (June)

Patriot (July)

John Fiske writes a new Yours Sincerely column every month in

New England Antiques Journal
Published by **Turley Publications**
24 Water Street, Palmer, MA 01069
Subscription information: 1.800.432.3505
www.antiquesjournal.com

Our readers tell us they read it cover-to-cover.